SEA HORSES

Maddie Gibbs

Maddie Gibbs

PowerKiDS press.

New York

Published in 2014 by The Rosen Publishing Group, Inc.
29 East 21st Street, New York, NY 10010

First Edition

Editor: Amelie von Zumbusch
Book Design: Andrew Povolny

Photo Credits: Cover Bill Kennedy/Shutterstock.com; p. 5 Hemera/Thinkstock; p. 7 Terence/Shutterstock.com; pp. 9, 11 Paul Zahl/National Geographic/Getty Images; p. 13 George Grall/National Geographic/Getty Images; p. 15 Secret Sea Visions/Paul Arnold/Getty Images; p. 17 iStockphoto/Thinkstock; p. 19 Wolfgang Poelzer/WaterFrame/Getty Images; p. 21 Kristina Vackova/Shutterstock.com; p. 23 Travel Ink/Gallo Images/Getty Images.

Library of Congress Cataloging-in-Publication Data

Gibbs, Maddie.
  Sea horses / by Maddie Gibbs. — First edition.
     pages cm. — (Powerkids readers. Fun fish)
  Includes index.
  ISBN 978-1-4777-0761-6 (library binding) — ISBN 978-1-4777-0855-2 (pbk.) —
  ISBN 978-1-4777-0856-9 (6-pack)
  1. Sea horses–Juvenile literature. I. Title.
  QL638.S9G485 2014
  597'.6798—dc23
                               2013001130

Contents

Sea horses are fish.

5

They have **snouts**.

A group is a **herd**.

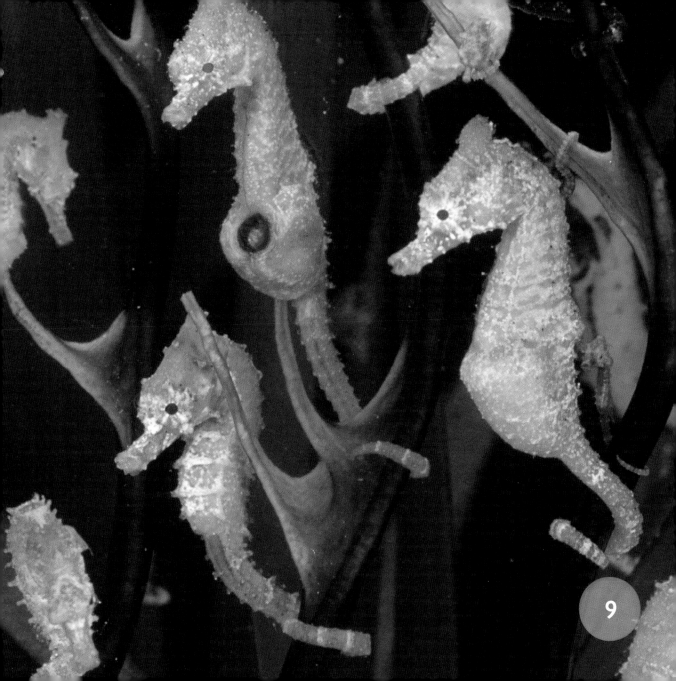

9

Males carry eggs. They give birth.

11

There are about 35 kinds.

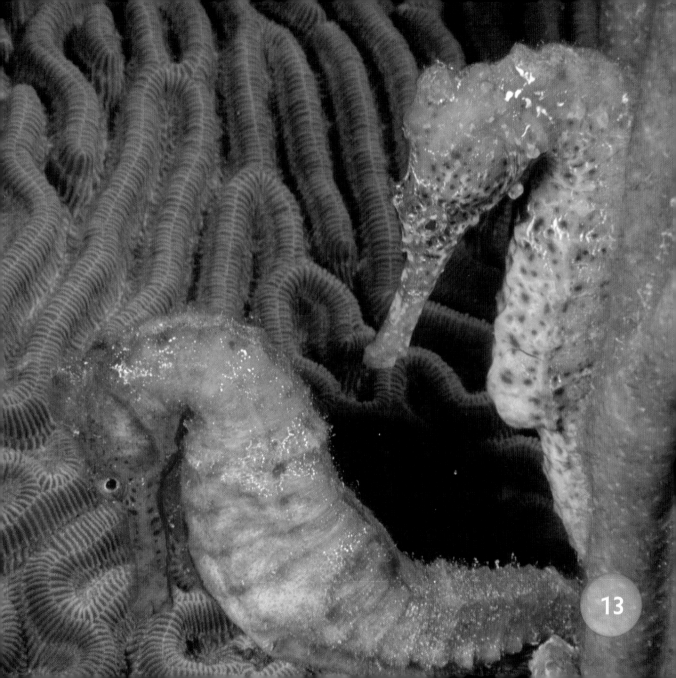

13

Zebra sea horses live near Australia.

15

Pygmy sea horses are the smallest.

17

Sea horses are slow.

19

They blend in to stay safe.

21

Can you spot one?

23

WORDS TO KNOW

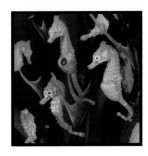  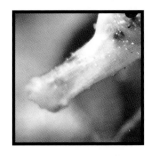

herd   sea horse   snout

INDEX

A
Australia, 14

E
eggs, 10

H
herd, 8

S
snouts, 6

WEBSITES

Due to the changing nature of Internet links, PowerKids Press has developed an online list of websites related to the subject of this book. This site is updated regularly. Please use this link to access the list:
www.powerkidslinks.com/pkrff/horse/